Born Nude

Nkwazi Mhango

Langaa Research & Publishing CIG
Mankon, Bamenda

Publisher
Langaa RPCIG
Langaa Research & Publishing Common Initiative Group
P.O. Box 902 Mankon
Bamenda
North West Region
Cameroon
Langaagrp@gmail.com
www.langaa-rpcig.net

Distributed in and outside N. America by African Books Collective
orders@africanbookscollective.com
www.africanbookscollective.com

ISBN-10: 9956-551-00-7

ISBN-13: 978-9956-551-00-2

Table of Contents

Acknowledgements

Nesaa my friend and consort
Thanks for your commitment and support
Ng'ani, Nkuzi and Nkwazi Jr. our children
Thanks for your company
This piece is yours and for you
It is your reminder though
We are here to pass
Yes
We need to leave good legacies
Comrade Pius Msekwa aka the *Rock* I salute you and
acknowledge you as a mentor and a friend
My brother and friend Ndugu Will Mutunga PhD
I envy you indeed
You two great people taught me humility
From you, I learned simplicity and human quality
On top of that, from you, I learned great humanity

Everybody Is Born Nude

Birth is everybody's exit to the world

Of all, people may differ

Really, one things is sure

None came with clothing on

Nobody can say this is a lie or delusion

Under the Sun, all were born completely nude

Defenceless, we were all born

Empty handed and nude all came to this world

Shall humans twig this setting life will be fa**b**

Denying being born nude will keep us in limb**o**

We need to remembe**r**

This rule of creatio**n**

Nudity is our origi**n**

We were not born like fug**u**

The fish whose poison is extremely feare**d**

Yet, their origin has remained the sam**e**

Nevertheless, Japanese makes it food

Weren't we made nude?

1

Ask the two that the nature joined
Your parents this comprehend
To it, science has testified
Whatever they enjoyed
Whatever they agreed
It is you they envisaged
Though their story is seldom told
The planters were totally nude
And the product came nude
We all were nude
Born nude

Swahili sage has it that
The one that hide's one's nudity will never have a baby
Everybody is born a baby
This is the only emblem we came with
Nobody was born king or queen
We were all born just nameless
We were born without titles
We picked everything in the world
We will leave everything behind
We all know this reality
Humans know it
Animals live it
Animals intuitively know it
Therefore, feel no guilty
We all were made nude
And we were equally born nude
Every animal and human is the product of nudity
Nudity is our link

The aim of this book is to define nudity as our link

To me, nudity is the emblem of equality
Our originality in nudity is the sign of our weakness
The weakness we equally all share
We share nudity regardless our diversity
So, too, we share humanity

Nobody is in the know though
As to how all of us will go
This is after we strode the world
The world we wrongly think we own
The world we take with high obsession
The world that ends up becoming an illusion
This is the world we found and will leave behind
Empty handed everybody will go
Surely, as we came we will go
Tycoons will go empty handed
They will leave everything behind

Just like paupers tycoons will do
Animals will go empty handed
Lucky them they owned nothing
Animals own nothing
As nude as we came
Lonely as we came
We, too, will leave empty handed
Lonely we will leave

Even twins will never leave together
Though they came together
Again, were they together?
Everybody had his or her own placenta
Like a plant's pistils
Every flower has its own petals

We all come disconnected from each other
We are only connected to our mothers

Nobody will go with his or her degrees
Nobody will take the pride of his or her pedigree
We all came without any degree
We arrive without knowing our pedigree
We didn't know our prestige
All we have made and treasured will be left here
Everything was found on earth
So, too, all will be left to mother earth

Nobody came with a bank account
Nobody came with a mansion or hut
We all came empty handed
So, too, we will abdicate
With songs and wails we will consent
As unaware as we came
Nobody knows when we will go

When the baby arrives
It is received by warm hands
It is the warm hands of its parents
The welcoming hand of midwives
Because we all understand
What the baby brings
We know how it is endowed
With our love and supports
We dress the baby
For, it comes nude
Nude everybody arrives

The baby is received by open hearts and hands
With clear and loving minds

4

The baby calls the world home
With the assistance of parents and the society
The baby puts its indelible marks on the world
Thought temporarily as it has always been
After finishing the mission
We will all equally go to where we came from
Do you know where that is?
Nobody knows

Before I was I wasn't
I didn't know I was
I will go back to this state
This is where I truly belong
Whenever I meditate
Sometimes, I refused to accepted
Yet, the truth will always stand
That I am here to pass

Philosophers and sages have tried to decipher this marvel
They have never gotten any near
Historians have chronicled everything
Always the end is missing
Who knows the beginning of everything?
Who knows the end of everything?
We know nothing
All we know is but speculate
All thinkers of the world have never gotten it

Religious people have stood above and speculated
Prophets had prophesied
Fake and real had the world inundated
Chroniclers had their isms documented
Thinking they know what we don't know
In the end,

They end up with beliefs
Why beliefs not proficiency?

Who controls and owns knowledge?
We all are knowledge seekers
We may think we know where we came from
Yet, we don't know where we head for
Despite this marvel
The key to the future
Is always in the past

In our mothers' wombs we were silent
In our tombs too we'll be quiet
Nothing will be a headache
Nothing will drive us crazy
In a grave we all enjoy equality
In a grave we all face the same predicament
Who knows what is next?
Dead people tell now stories
If so, why should we live in worries?

Some talk about glory
Others talk about purgatory
All is nothing but vainglory
All is nothing but demagoguery
Again, who knows?
I want to see whoever knows
To know how he or she knew it
I want to know all he or she knows

Some feel are better than others
Some think are more beautiful than others
Are there truly who are better than others?
Who are we to lie to ourselves like this?

Aren't animals better than us?
Look at them
They don't oft-take shower
They don't vie for power
Animals are not corrupt
They don't do all dirty things humans do?

Humility is the best human quality
Beauty is always inside humanity
We are all beautiful
We are all to be to each other bountiful

My admission

I must admit and say it from the outset
That I have always been in the quest
It is the quest for reality
That is based on equality
Equality of the entire humanity
That is what has been my quest
From my experience and curiosity
From my thirst for familiarity
I am revisiting our originality
I do this with sincerity
Too, with humbleness and humility I write
Equality is what I swoop
Yes, equality is our only loop

Admittedly, I don't know everything; however, what I know
has something in it
This is why I am questioning everything as I seek light and
reality
I am dwelling on somethings that are trivialised and faultily
treated
I am touching on the nature and the origin of all humanity
Regardless of race and creed, I explore humanity
Regardless their pigments of their skins or the creeds of their
cultures and creed
I am dealing with all humanity in its totality
I touch on human weakness and vanity
Surely, I am delving into human susceptibility

The confusion humanity faces is built in their mind-sets
Much is the result of rigidity
As it gyrates around conceit
Greatness is their quest

9

Everybody wants to be mightier
Though he or she knows he or she is weaker

Confusion is nothing but the way they look at themselves and
others
Egoistically some humans may think they are better than
others
Realistically, nobody is better than others
We all are but mortals
Our mortality doesn't know our puny bubbles
The opium that makes some people think they are better than
others

Who is better among humans?
Aren't they the humble ones?
Show me who is better than all of us
He or she who did not came nude
To me the best are those who accept human weakness
Better are those who accept human equivalence

What makes us different and unequal is nothing but the
lenses we use
Though this doesn't bother many of us
However it has produced many victims
I have decided to take this difficulty by choice
I want to make things straight
Too, I will elucidate on human assets
As they revolve around polemics
I want to unearth all gimmicks
Cardinal one being human originality
Let me state it from the onset
The time we venture into this troubling world
To which we all arrive nude
Aren't we coming nude?

Indeed, we all were born nude

There are important things we trivialise
We trivialise big things
Yet, we make trivial things big
The very things we overlook and oppose
We discuss tonnes of sciences
We philosophise molds of arts and politics
In the end, we end up with theatrics
We embark on micro and mega economics
Yet, we forget our crescendos
Talking about them gets innuendos
These are the very things
This tome addresses
This is the very essence
That this book touches on the crux
As to how we came to this world
We all arrived nude

Our bodies were nude
Our brains were nude
Our eyes were hemianopia
Means our vision was not clear
What we knew it is only myopia
We were empty
Just like vessels
We were just nude

Even for twins it didn't matter who came first
It didn't make any difference from who came last
They all were thirsty
They needed their mother to slake their thirsty
They were all hungry and thirsty
Everything was clumsy

11

The midwives had to hide us
All in all, we all came nude
Like everybody, we came nude

We were born innocent
Just like a tabula rasa or a blank slate
However, everybody was born with a big heart
Mundanely, we were all perfect
Things though did change
When we entered the world of age
This is the very age of habitual triage
Despite all, we were born nude

When we arrived, we were blameless
Ours were nothing but shrieks and helplessness
To overlook such important and mind-bending things
We tend to condemn and avoid discussing nudity
Who wants to talk about nudity?
Nudity is subject to taboos
It is always pushed under the carpet
Again, the fact remains
It always tiptoes
Weren't we born nude?

I must say this categorically
I am not a nudist
Instead, I am for equality
Nudity I pursue is about our originality
It is about our equality as humanity

He or she who was born out of sexual intercourse will never
be better than others
Whether you were born conjugally or otherwise
The same will always apply to you

12

You were born nude
As well, you will all leave this world
Sorrows are the only thing people will exude
As one exits this confusing world
The fact will remain that you came nude

Whether you are a tycoon or a pauper, the road is the same
Whether you are a professor or doctor, the manner is the
same
We will all die; this has no qualms at all
Death is for us all
We who were born nude

We came with water and blood
Those are the only things we arrived with
We were received by caring hands
The mightier hands of the midwives
Came the might hands of our mothers
The mighty protection of our fathers
The mighty ever-watching eyes of our parents
The mightier eye of the society
From them we continued with our lives
We all came nude

Show me who came clean
Or the one whose mother didn't suffer pains
We came all covered in blood
We all had an umbilical cord
This is our first source of food
Before we came to this world
Our mothers' wombs fed us
In their wombs we grew and throve
We were nourished by their exceptional love
From their commitment we were made

From their vows we were germinated
Hail all mothers

We are all born toothless
Our mothers used to chew for us
Some of us will die toothless
We were powerless
We, indeed, were harmless
We are all born sinless
Though we die in many messes
Are sins real or human creation?
Here come religions
Innocent as they always are
Babies are indoctrinated in our dogmas
They are taught to feel guilty without any iniquities
Though equal they came to the world
Slowly we start teaching them inequalities
Some teach them racism
Some teach them egoism
All isms kick in
Their blamelessness slowly wanes

Whatever that is better for us as parents
Becomes better for them
We teach them our *realism*
We teach them capitalism and consumerism
We teach them extremism and nihilism
Innocent babies that came nude
Some end up dressed in messy outfits
It is because of acquired artificial and fake isms
Thanks to this blindness, the world now faces schisms
Accuse it of racism
Some colours are eulogised
Others are demonised

What will never be changed is
We all came nude
We may glorify our colours
What will we do with our blood?
We may deify our pedigree
What of our shared destiny

Nobody is born with deviltry
We were all born holy
Nobody was born with criminality
We were all born clean and neat
We were born without any identity
Ours was nothing but humility
We are born without any sin or guilt
We weren't born with the original sin
I refuse to buy into this irrationality
Its logic is so thin
We are born innocent
The world turns us into inchoate
All we know is nudity
All we know is our vanity
We who were born nude

Isn't original sin a fallacy?
Some say original sin is nothing but idiocy
How can an innocent baby sin
Isn't this thing original sin human fabrication?
Is it not a tool for domination?
Isn't the original sin is ungodly thing?
We all were born equal
There was nothing sexual
We born of the womb
Our hearts will stop to throb
There will come the end of our hobnob

Everybody will become a blob
No more aplomb
We will all end in the tomb

All beliefs will become obsolete
All such garbage is nothing
But monkey business
No original or secondary sin
Nobody knows what will be our end

Men and women were all born equal
But the world turned them unequal
Biology set them apart
The society so, too, created   a rift
They all blessed sexual disparity
This is the source of all evils
Inequality is the work of the devils
The devils of this world
Whatever you call it
Social construction
Patriarchy hegemony
It is still evil
For, it bedevilled our natural arrangement

None is better than another
I openly tell thee
The best of humanity is he or she
The one whose comportment is nice
The one who respects humanity
Like trees we are identified by our fruits
Like flowers we are introduced by our colours and scents

As humans, we must be recognised for our equality
We all must be defined by our humanity
The best among us is the one whose virtue is humility
This virtue has no any ambiguity
Born nude and death define our equality
Our needs as well portrays our equality

We were all born with true love
We are the creatures and products of love
We need to keep and spread this love
Every baby is an iron in a velvet globe
However, as we grow hate creeps in
Animal instincts kick in
Up until, we naturally and sheepishly go to the grave
Many will have already committed many sins
They will hate one another
They will fight one another
This is our destiny
Those who were born nude
Why is the black soil fertile?
Why birds like black seeds?

Born without baggage

We were born without any allegiance to any creeds
Be it crescents or crosses
We did not know parties and creeds
We did not know anything about our races
We were all human creatures
We didn't know the difference between tyranny
We did not know democracy
Ours, in fact, was nothing but true innocence
We knew neither religion nor politics
We were born nude and neutral

I want somebody to truthfully tell me
Who is better among humans?
It has never crossed my mind
When it comes to racially different humankind
Is it the one that thinks is better than others
Or the ones that equally treat others?
Is human good quality the product of colour or good deeds?
Don't we have humans who are like animals?
Whose actions are despicable and horrendous?
Be they black or white
Such humans are but second-rate
Be they wealthy or unfortunate
Such humans are beasts
Maybe, if we talk of inequities
We should mean such brutes

We came without any political luggage or revel

We knew no difference between Marxism and capitalism
We were not captives or slaves of dogmatism
We knew no euphemism
We came without any sense of sarcasm
Ours was nothing but humanism
We worshipped neither a cross nor a crescent
We were born pure at heart
We were innocent in every aspect
We knew no apostles or prophets
We knew no deities
We did not know even our ancestors
We were just little creatures
That struggled in our realms
What for if we were sinless?
What for if we were unconscious?
We knew no bigotry
We knew no partiality
All are the baggage we got here on the soil
Those who put us in this turmoil
Didn't bother about our future intellectualism
They didn't even think about our antagonism

Some allegedly say their ways of life are better than others
With such misguided pretext they demonise others
Ironically, they forget one reality
That all humans enjoy human parity
If all humans are equal
All cultures or ways of life must be equally equal
Cultures are like plants in a beautiful lea
Their beauty becomes clear
When they are standing together

If each is taken away from others
The beauties too disappear
All cultures and ways of life bear two sides
They all have good and bad sides
And, indeed, this is a cardinal rule

Some colonise others
Under this fake superiority they abuse and rob others
They call such a crime civilisation
What type of civilisation
What civilisation is this?
This is nothing but narcissism
There is only one name
One can give such a crime
This is nothing but insanity

Some came with their ever-bullying religions
They said they are the way to salvation
They hid everything from our appreciations
They used them to destroy others' way
To end up finding themselves in repression
If there is anything they brought
It is nothing but destruction

They said they knew and know God
Have they ever shown their God?
Whose God is visible?
Whose God is reachable?
Isn't God a fable?
Call it him or her, infamous or noble
God will always remain a puzzle

Up until people stop pretending they know him or her
Nobody knows God more than others
When it comes to who God is, we are all but fumblers

How many swindlers and pretenders litter the world?
They preach lies and their netherworld
Those who lie they were sent by God
They call such lies the words of God
Which God?
Is it the God of fire or ardour?
If God is everywhere at any and every moments
Why should he or she send agents?

Nevertheless
We all are dependent on each other
The poor makes the rich richer
In some cases, the richer makes the poor poorer
What we do in this temporal life of ours
Aren't our lives like bubbles?
Better life is nothing but exchanging our gifts of nature
Nobody can sail through alone; and reach the destination
The pilot doesn't fly a plane alone
He has people behind the scene
It is only the birds and their savviness
They fly without radars
They have nobody to tell them about the weather
They do everything alone
Nevertheless, we look down at them
While we learned the science of flying from them
Aren't birds and insects greater aviators?
Aren't they our teachers?

What of fish that taught us navigation?
What of ants that taught us the science of building houses?
Aren't these simple creatures our partners in our lives?

Everybody needs a partner
It makes one's life warmer and better
It is the perfection of life that we seek in such partnerships
It is only the fulfillment of life we find in this arrangement
Without it we all face hardships
Without it, our lives are neither fulfilled nor complete
We need the progenies to take over from us
We need to see the image the creator hid in us
Who dispute this noble prearrangement?
Aren't our progenies the reflection of our equality?
Aren't our needs the expression of our vulnerability?

Aren't all creatures programmed?
How many things do we do but we can't offer
Any explanation?
Aren't humans ignorant of many things around and afar from
them?
Nobody is born wise and knowledgeable
He or she who hates knowledge
He or she will be exploited by those with knowledge
Again, knowledge is like a gun
Knowledge is a very powerful weapon
It all depends on how one uses it
Some use it to destroy others
While others use it to help others
The knowledge that destroys
Is as good as poison

Nobody should have it
For, having it is nothing but a loss
Having destructive knowledge is nothing but sufferings

Destructive wealth is like a disease
It kills those who own it
You are wealthy not because you are smart
One is poor not because is indolent
There is a big lesson in this trait
We need to examine it and solve its mystery
Again, this needs sincerity and bravery

Don't take pride in your affluence
Never take pride in your supremacy
The powerful depend on the powerless
For, he or she who gives the power
He or she is the same who denies it to others
By the way, is power something timeless?
Power comes and goes
Humanity always remained
Power always deceives
Humanity always does justice

How many dictators the world has ever seen
Where are they now
Didn't their powers destroy them?
Didn't their powers abandon them?
Interestingly, powers left them when they needed them
Didn't they misuse their powers to destroy others?
What is power if its end is the trail of destruction?

What's the importance of power that corrupts?
What's power that destroys who wages it?
Better to have no power and be safer
Than having power and become a monster

All human are equal
Ask those dictators or read their history
Didn't they crave love?
Didn't they yearn for security?
They caused all calamities
Their aim was to be secured
However, they were vulnerable
Simply because they were proud
They were ignorant and blind
Who wants such power?
The power of destruction
The power of obliteration

We all longed for our mothers' warmth
We cried for their love and faith
It needs only love and faith
To take on this labour of love
Under and above, it is not just love
It needs sacrifice and true love
It is because of love
All of us made it through
It is the love of our mothers
The love of our fathers
Jointly they invested in us
To end up feeling proud
For whatever we achieve

Parents' love is second to none
It is always unlimited given
Nothing is expected of the recipient
If there is anything expected
It is nothing but humanity
Do it to your parents or others
This is always what is theirs

Our mothers cleaned our dirty butts
They washed our feet
They brushed our teeth
More importantly though
They didn't complain
They have never complained
They will never complain
They have never demanded any payment
Who can estimate such payments?
Who can replicate what we got from our parents?

Who can count the hugs and kisses he or she got from
parents
Didn't they cuddle you in their chests?
For those who don't want to have children
How will they pay such second-to-none treatments?
Are we beasts that cannot see such love
Is there anything we need over and above?

Even beasts are sometimes better
They appreciate the love of their parents
Despite knowing a little

Beasts still love their parents
They always love each altogether
This is why a lion doesn't eat the meat of another

Our parents made us ship-shape
All the while were under their guardianship
They made us feel secure and happy
At certain time, they taught us everything
They sacrificed everything
They paid our school fees
They settled our health bills
They worked like bees
To see us achieve everything
Some were not educated
Yet, they sent us to school
They stood by us and saw us through
We became professors
Others became doctors
Others become janitors
While others become offenders
This is not the fault of our parents though
What can we pay our mentors?
Our dear parents

Do you remember what they taught you?
Do you appreciate what they invested in you?
You asked them about almost everything
They simplistically and softly taught everything
This is before you grew up to rebel against their knowledge
You are now your own sage
Yet, the truth reminds

They build your foundation

Your parents gave you your name
They stood by you in fame and shame
You grew up and used their name
They have never asked you to redress them

Do you remember how you marvelled almost about
everything?
They taught you about the stars
You wanted to touch the Sun
You wanted to own the Moon
They opened your universe
Can you tell why the world is the reflection of the universe?
Go interrogate everything
Do you know why all tree stems are like they are?
Almost everything reflects the unknown universe
Go look at trees' stems
They are either in star shapes if not globular
Do you know why?

Do you remember when you touched fire?
Uh, you thought it was a cool thing
Remember the numbness of cold water
Do you remember when you felt hungry?
Did you understand what it was?
Everything was a wunderkind
You chased the birds
Thinking you would catch them
Did you know how smart they are?

Do you remember?
You once believed that parents knew everything
This is before you concluded they knew a few things
You ended up believing they know nothing
You termed them archaic
Yet, you made a U-turn
You believed in their old wisdom
Too late though

Try to remember
How many times they kissed you
Nobody can count how many times they hugged you
How many times did they lose their sleeps for you?
Remember how they listened to you
It is at the time your sounds did not make sense
You were just blabbling
Despite that, they listened to you
Do you listen to them?

Do you remember how they supported you?
It is when you were trying to walk
You used to wobble
Yet, they taught you how to walk
You used to blabber
They taught you how to talk
What will you teach them?

They spent their youthhood on you
Will you spend yours on them?
They gave you everything precious they had
Will you equally reciprocate?

Can you pay their labour of love?
It is upon you to decide
Betray them
Your kids will pay for them
They will, as well, betray you
They will give you exactly the same

Many blindly sink in their reverie
They even abandon the crappie
About and for nonsense they vie
They even forget the day they will die
They forget the moxie
With which their parents fended for them
To make them who they are today
What an injury!

Without your loving parents
Of course, caring parents
Protective parents
Sacrificing parents
You would not have become who you are
Even those that are with you
They would not have been with you
Without them you'd not been where you are
You are what and who you are
It is because of your selfless parents

They might have some glitches
Yet, for the fact, they fought for you
Don't think they are seraphs
They are but humans

They have their weakness
Yet, they have their strengths
To make you who you are
Yes, they sacrificed for you
Your parents truly listened to you
When everything was silent
As you kicked in your mother's womb
They just listened with aplomb
Even when everything was turbulent
They listened patiently
As you hit the ground crying
As the hands of the midwives received you
They just went on listening
Even when you started making sense of things
They still listened

They started teaching you
Whatever important they inculcated in you
You became who you are now
Just because your parents listened
It is just because your parents understood
It is just because your parents sacrificed
They were always there when needed
And they generously provided

Our parents cared a lot about us
Do we, as well, care a lot about them?
They offered the best they had
Do you offer the best to them?
When you were sick they listened
You cried they listened

You were angry they listened
You were hungry they too listened
They comforted you
They fed you
They lulled you
`   They lived for you
Are you now living for them?

Your parents knew when you needed what
They knew when you were thirsty
They surely and timely knew when you were hungry
They knew the type of food you needed
They provided even when you did not ask
They were always there from dawn to dusk
Your life became their full time job
Do you still remember this?

Try to remember where your parents took you from
Remember all risks they took for you
Do you do the same to them?
Are they as important to you as you were to them?
These are the questions you always need to ask
To them you need to provide answers

Some were not educated
Yet, they educated their children
Some were poor
Then they prayed all success for their children
Can such roles be paid for?

Who is better than others?

Humans are born nude
They are all born needy
Whose mouth smells perfumes every morning?
Who does not brush his or her teeth every morning and
evening?
It isn't only the baby whose mouth smells aroma?
Thought the baby doesn't eat gourmet
What lesson does such nature put across?
Don't we all have weaknesses?
This is what it means to be human

We were all born humble, valuable and vulnerable
We were born to launch a struggle
Yes, a struggle for dear life
Some wins high life
Others ended up with normal life
Others die in a miserable life
This is life
Life nobody can accurately define

Despite different stations in life
We all live life
Interestingly others cut their lives short
Others treasure this gift
While others take it as a right
Is life really a right?
To me, life is but a gift

We indeed are equal physically and biologically
Whose heart is in the right side of the body but not the left?

Our parents teach used us good things
They always teach us to separate good things from bad things
Where then do we get bad things?
Whom can we blame this on?
And whom can we credit all for?
Some said the world is not bad
Instead humans make it bad
If this is the case then
Where do we put people who do virtuous things?

Our parents gave us the best they were able to offer
Better education formal and informal
Though not all were able to meet this
They offered their best

Our parents taught us hygiene and cleanliness
Yet, when some grew thought are cleaner than their parents
When they see wrinkles on their parents' faces
They think they didn't have smooth faces
They look down at them
Remember this is the nature of things
They were as young and attractive as anybody
Everybody under the sun will one day go the same way
Aging is a judicious agent for us
Never abandon your parents
Never look them down
You are who you are because of them
It is the matter of time you will join them

You will see wrinkles on your face
Your organs will stop taking your orders
You will feel unsayable burden on your shoulders

Some robbed others to offer their children a good education
Some ate badly in order to build good foundations
They did all these because of their progenies
Is it right to abandon them at the hour of need?
How many are imprisoning their parents in senior homes?
How many do not have time to visit them in these homes?
Who care about the negligence and loneliness they may face?
Do you seek their consents to confine them in such homes?
If you live by sword, you will die by sword
Your children will confine you there as a reward
For what you did to your parents

I have never seen a nest for senior birds
Neither have I seen the den for senior beasts
Again, beasts are not hominids
Maybe, they care about their elders
If they don't do
They are but beasts
They have no conscience like humans
Even so, they have a lot to teach us

I am not judging saying this is unfair
I don't mean to badmouth anybody
However, I must admit it
Treat everybody the way you would like to be treated
Put yourself in the shoes of confined parents and consider
Examine it; and see if it is fair

Always, the spear is good for the hog
For a human it is throbbing
Never let your parents suffer in despair
Return them what they gave you
Appreciate and celebrate whatever they did to you
You came absolutely nude
They fully dressed you
You came crying
They calmed you down
You came hungry
They fed you
What else do you want?
As the saying goes
Love begins with love
It must end with love
Love your parents

Some parents pay even for the marriage of their children
Ironically, some children's wives antagonise their in-laws
Is this the way one has to pay for such bigheartedness?
Parents' love has no limits
However, many take it for granted
Some grandparents take good care of their grandchildren
This is wonderful to perform
It creates a strong bond among them
This is what we inherited from our ancestors
Our parents are always supportive
Especially at our early stages
They want us to have a very happy life
Better life than theirs
They sacrifice everything for the sake of our happiness

They do whatever they can for success
They celebrate their children's success as theirs
The lesson here is simple and sure
If you sow wind, you will reap whirlwind
If you sow mustard, you will reap mustard
If you sow hatred, you will reap hatred
Treat others the way you would like to be treated

Teach our children mannerism
Save them from materialism
Avert them individualism
We are destroying the world
Selfishness has become a scourge for this world
Everybody thinks about him or herself
This way we cannot develop
If we do
It is materially but not morally
This is why global warming is looming

Fish taught us to swim
Do we complement them?
We think we know more than they do
Do we really do?
We study them
Do we know if they study us?
Who cares to investigate such issues?
Now we need to interrogate everything
Think about this without any ado
You will see how things work
Importantly, we must concede
We all were born nude

Who didn't wear diapers?
Who didn't wet beds?
Who remembers the taste and sweetness of mother's milk?
Do you know how many litres of milk you sucked from your
mother?
Is there anything you can compare with your mother?
The nurse who saw you through healthy and safely
The guard who made you confident and safer
The entertainer who made you happier
What a mystery that we overlook!
What a great lesson we take for granted
We all gave our parents sleepless nights

When we were sick
They forsook their sleeps
Everything was put on a stop
To see to it we get well
Is there any child that doesn't yell?
Show me one
I will respect her or him
We all went through the same penchant
Crawling became our art
Picking objects became our trait
Nudity became our identity
For, we all arrived nude

We came in the same manner and way
We, too, will follow the same way
The pattern for all human is the same
It may differ in names
Yet, it is the same

Some are destined to die at early age
While others will attain full age
Nobody can change anything
We cannot add or reduce
What is presaged endures
It is as it is
We just slink in it
Ours has always been to wait
Whatever the fate has in store for us
Like it was for our nudity
So is our endpoint
We were born nude

Nobody will be great
Anybody born of semen
The product of menstruation
Isn't menstruation regarded as a forbidden one?
Is it subject to any open discussion?
Isn't it treated like an abomination?
Ironically, we love its creation!
What greatness can such a person have?
What of the one that sired him or her
What of the one that carried him or her in her womb
All that came from the womb will end in the tomb
Who is the hero here?
Consider how gametes meet drupes
Where do they reside
Aren't they are neighbouring to urine and faeces
What greatness can come from such a creature?
How while it was made out of nudity
How if it has come nude

I see some people making fuss
What for is your ruckus
Do you think you have anything extraordinary?
Poor them and you
Some want to be treated exceptionally
Wherever they go is but chaos
They think they are the high and the mighty
They want to be noticed and revered
Even when they know they are mere mortals
Mere immoral mortals that can vanish in the blink of an eye
Some don't even have any shuteye
They are always thinking about rarity
The exceptionality they want is but a mist
Sure, everything they treasure is temporal
They forget one thing really
All human were born nude

All human were born nude
We all came confused and crying
We are accompanied by our tears
Even when we die
Others shed tears for us
This is the rule of the nature
It is a true biological culture
It is for every creature
That comes from a woman's womb
The very creature
Yes, the one whose destiny is the catacomb
Is there any baby that comes to the world laughing?
Truly, I am not kidding
I am not even dreaming or trying to make things unassuming

All baby come nude

All babies arrive alike
All stages they go through are alike
They are always accompanied by tears
Theirs has always been fury and fears
They learn how to lark
They are taught how to talk
They learn how to walk
All of all and above all
Yet, crying is one thing everybody came with
Crying too is the same thing we will live with
From nudity we were made
Nude we arrived

Otherwise we are but nobody
Kings were born nude
Prophets were born nude
Billionaires were born nude
Paupers were born nude
Jesus was born nude
Mohammad was born nude
Holy people were born nude
You too were born nude
I too was born nude
Men were born nude
Women were born nude
They were all born out of nudity

Is there who can plant without digging?
Is there any seed that can germinate without watering?

41

Every seed germinates from the process of rotting
From something feeble we get something strong
This is the same to everything
Seeds must shed their coats to germinate

Everything has its life span on this earth
When times to expire arrives, it will fade
Unceremoniously everything will vanish
Others will perish
This is a cardinal principle
This is the Truth
Hold your breath!
Everything will come to an end
Though, nobody knows when it is the end
He or she who came nude
Shall come to an end

Mortals are like leaves on a tree
All leaves will one day dry
Thereafter they will fall
Everything will fly away
Ours is a stint
Hear me thee
Our lives are not our right
They are but a gift
Enjoy it peacefully
Live is humanly

Who knows?

Who knows where we go
Do we know where we came from?
Go ask historians
They will speculate
Ask boffins
They will estimate
Despite all such
Nobody knows surely
Where we came from
We who came nude

Bees and butterfly know the secrets of plants
Do plants know theirs?
Some snakes are poisonous
Yet, they are killed by capons
Despite their antagonism
They all lay spawns
Miraculously, they are from different kinds
Differently from us
They came with their defence
The calves aren't smarter than human babies?
Look at goat's kids
They get out of the womb and walk
How long does it take for human to reach such a landmark?

Despite such hopelessness
Humans still feel better than them
Have you ever seen a crocodile breastfeeding?

Birds too don't breastfeed
Aren't their babies smart than ours
Who interrogate this secret?
Who bothers to separate facts from myths?
Acid is but a *monger tout or* that eats everything
Yet, it is put in weak containers
Take plastics
Don't they contain acids?
Like slipperiness
It brings tough stuff down easily
Don't elephant fear bees?
Look at their sizes
Aren't there many lessons?
All depends on how we view things

You can fight all battles
Nonetheless, you can't win all battles
You will win some
As well, you will lose some
This is the principle
All have to embrace
There is nothing new in this
Importantly, we need to realise
We are equally created
This is why we were all born nude

Nobody is born free
We are born with helplessness
This is why we need somebody to care for us
Is the baby really free?
Is the parent really free?

They all depend on each other
The parents need a baby
The baby too, depend on the parents
He or she was born nude
Nudity is the only thing he or she owned

Babies have never been born free
They are born innocent
There is a difference between innocence and freedom
People confuse innocence and freedom
Some are delivered and abandoned
Others are heartlessly killed
Others are aborted
They call this pro-choice
Whose choice is this?
Who has to make this choice?
Do they ask the victims who know nothing?
Despite all that, they are all born nude

Animals don't procure abortions
They take care of their progenies
To them choice is only one, to take care of their babies
Yet, some humans are worse than animals
They kill their zygotes
They starve their babies
Some don't even breastfeed them
While they themselves were breastfed

Some ladies value more their tits than their babies
Nevertheless, they call these human rights
Are they real human rights?

Whose rights are these?
Between the rights of the one who has power over another
And the one who is totally helpless
Despite this callomania
Nothing will stand the test of time
On their last days, they will all be helpless

I feel saddened and sickened these days
I see many condemning breastfeeding
What used to be pride is now relegated to ignominy
Women are no longer allowed to breastfeed wherever they
deem fit
Some societies are shunning them while other are imposing
fines them
What has the world recently become?
Since when breastfeeding became a shame
Ironically, while those condemning breastfeeding make it a
sin
They make do with sacrilegious things such as tattoos and
nudity
Who is supposed to be condemned between the one
breastfeeding and the one kissing publicly?
Who is supposed to be fined between the one feeding the
baby
And the one that is showing bad manners publicly

Cows and goats feed publicly
Are animals' babies better than humans'?
Animals' babies are fed whenever mothers decide
What is wrong with humans who do not allow such a right?

Ironically, child-breastfeeding haters aren't perturbed by baby
commodes?
We need to let children and mothers enjoy their feeding and
being fed right

I remember I was told
That when I was young
My parents looked after me
Up until, I became who I am
I became my own witness
I remember my parents' care and love
This is my treasure trove
However, things have changed
Children are now abandoning their elderly parents
Without remembering how they exploited them
They forgot all that their parents did for them
They call this development
Is this really development
Call it insanity
This is nothing but wickedness
That harbours selfishness
Nonetheless, we cannot dispute it
That we were all born nude

Show me who will never age
Whose body will never negate
Though we see and know all this
We tend to forget for our own peril
With our illusions we create our own hell
We create an abyss
Yet, we call it a paradise

Just because we are such heartless illiterates
Illiterates of what we need to know naturally
We were all born nude

Nobody came with a name
We all came unnamed
Nobody came with the fame
We all came plain
We came unarmed
We all got our names from the world
We too will leave them in the same world
Nobody knows who he or she will become
All the same
Nobody knows about time
The time this world will cease to be our home
One thing we are sure of is that this world is not our home

Some animals are born clothing on
Goats and cows know this too well
They are born with their suits on
Yet, they don't pretend to be better
They don't even know or care
They don't laugh at us who were born nude
Maybe, these are smart
Interestingly, they make no deal out it
As for humans
Whether you are highly educated
Or you are heavily indebted
Even if you are richer and smarter
We all were born nude
We all came to this world

Likewise, we will leave it behind

Sometimes, animals are better than humans
All their lives
They don't fight over eternity
They don't fight over property
They know of no toothpaste
They don't use toilet papers
They use no perfumes
Yet, they don't smell yuck
Look at their teeth
They are always sparking
Smell their bodies
They are always amusing
What of humans?
What a mess!

Animals are realistic
They have never labour under any theatrics
They don't fight over eternity
They don't fight over property
Though we think their lives are boring
Actually, they are always amusing

Some xenophobes hide behind the pigments of their skins
They commit all sorts of sins
They turn other humans into things
We call this commodification
Others call it objectification
They give colour wrong and misleading connotations
White has always been a trendy colour of all

Racism has been offered a dais
When you look at the true meaning of colour
White vanishes in the fog
Yet, blind racists still do it with glib
Though what is said to be white ends up being a fib

Do different spots on goats make them different?
How many do look at this arrangement?
A cow may be black or white
Yet, no cow thinks it is different
White cow is not better than a black one
Black chicken is not better than a white one
But when it comes to humans
Colour, not blood, becomes an in thing
How mediocre humans are

Despite their differences in complexions and heights
Nobody has ever differentiated trees based on discriminatory
trait
Again, when it comes to humans, all changes abruptly
This shows how racism is hallucination and unfamiliarity
How can creature born nude be different?

Our colours have nothing to do with our worthy
Our colours have nothing to do with our unworthiness
What defines us is nothing but the contents of our
comportments
We may have different pigments on our skin
However, we have one same thing that is blood
All humans have red blood
The numbers of blood cells are the same

The types of blood groups are the same
The numbers of organs are the same
We are all the same
We who were born nude

Some hide behind sexual orientation
They say women are weak and wicked
Again, when I look at all men
I end up being shocked
All men came from the women's womb
Isn't this fab?
All women are sired by men
Like all men are conceived by women
Who is who then?
This signifies our equality
I sire you
You give birth to me

Men don't know even their fathers
They only know them from their mothers
Even their fathers don't know if they really are their fathers
They all depend on their mothers
Can such creatures be treated like no-brainers?
While they are the harbingers of our being
Many call themselves sons of men
Aren't they sons of women
I would say they are sons and daughters of all
Taking one and leaving another is impertinence

Men without women won't function
Women without men won't procreate

They both depend on each other
None better than another
The best ones are those that are equal
Those who are equal regardless their gender differentiations

Whose language is ascribed to a person as the first one knows
It is obvious the mother language
Where is the father language?
Even when it comes to where we belong
Mother still features high
The only planet we have is not spared in this challenge
It is called mother earth
Where is father earth?
Apart from that there is Mother Nature
Where is father nature?
You can go as far as motherland
This means where someone was born
When it comes to fatherland
It denotes one's patriotism!
Does mean mothers are not patriotic
Are the fathers, means males, only patriotic?
This is where patriarchal systems lie
What a big lie!

Wasn't this lie of fatherland created by Nazis?
Why are we still using it currently?
How many interrogate such lies critically
Aren't many still labouring under and harbouring such lies?
However, this is not so unusual
Humans have the tendency of siding with the powerful
As they give a wide berth to the less powerful

Guess what

When a baby starts to talk, starts with the word mom
This has unique wisdom
How many look at this wisdom as it is?
How many have ever been bothered with this
Neither scientists nor philosophers
They all overlook this mystery

Don't babies teach us something?
Who care to learn from them?
Why start with mom but not dad?
Isn't this simple evidence?
That we have so many things to learn yet

Some people are socially constructed as fatherless
Never had I seen a person who is motherless
Maybe, those cloned in the laboratories
Laboratory kids will have no mothers
As they will do with fathers

Is there any person who came from one person?
Show me one
They say Jesus did
Again, such are old stories
In reality, everybody is the product of two
Isn't this a balancing act of nature?
Isn't this the law of equality?

All humans are equal however unequal they can be made to
believe and behave
We need to stand by this creed and be brave
All bees are equal in their beehive
So, too, all hyenas are equal in the cave
This is how we were created by the power above
Yes, the one that made us come nude

Some people hide behind their blood line
Some say are of the royal line
Nonsense
Where do we go when we die?
Is there any royal line in the purgatory?
Aren't we indoctrinated that in the heaven all are equal?
Life of mightiness is but a lie
Will you live forever?
Where were you before you were born?
Nobody knows this unknown
Aren't we always afraid of the unknown?
Again, there is still a tryst of such idiocy
Stop such mediocracy
It is but mere lunacy
Better to stop this intellectual lethargy
It won't take us anywhere except to the ill destiny
Killing and robbing each other with impunity
Discriminating against each other with immunity
Based on international complicity and gullibility
The lunacy of thinking you are better than others
It is a self-denunciation to discriminate against others
Weren't you born nude?

Where will you go after dying?
I am sure you know nothing
Aren't you going to be entombed in the womb of mother
earth?
Aren't you going to become dust in the crust of mother
earth?
Who then is better than another if we all go the same way?
What value does it have the creature that came nude?
We all came nude

When death slinks in for us, we shrink
What it leaves back is nothing but shock
About it we collectively talk
We internalise the aftershock
Is there anybody who doesn't complain about death?

Show me anybody who isn't afraid of death
Generals fear death
Priests fear death
No general no coward
No fighter no underdog
Before ruthless death nobody is spared
We all are vulnerably concerned
As if it is not enough
When a pain kicks in, we all shriek
When the thunderbolt roars
We all seek shelters
Let us loudly think
Don't let your eye to wink
Aren't we equally weak?
As nude we were born

As vulnerable we truly will remain

Who knows what happens when a person passes on
Don't we live and believe in speculations
Some say there will be fire on the day of conclusion
Some assuredly say there will be delight
Who went there and came back to tell us the stories?
Dead people tell no stories

Some want to be emulated as nobles
They conceal their frailties behind nobleness
Which noble person can exploit others?
What kind of nobility that allows a person to discriminate
against others
Is this nobility or fallacy

What do you do in your lavatories?
Do you plant any seed there?
Do your faeces smell perfumes?
Why then cheating yourselves
Don't your mouths smell horrifically in the morning?
If yes, then, you're truly exceptionally noble

From the womb to the ossuary
Humans are sufferers
Animals have no tombs in which to be entombed
Yet, if you look at their lives
Sometimes, they are better than hominids
Since coming out their mothers' wombs
Animals never brush their teeth
Yet, they don't smell horribly

They never have daily showers
Yet, they don't smell despondently
What of humans with our pride and superiority
Isn't it vainglory?
Isn't it this our perfunctory
Isn't such comportment nugatory?

The song of equality

Now let me exclusively talks about a woman
When I talk about a woman
I talk about the cathedral of human life
Don't take offence in this
When I say the cathedral of life
I seriously mean it
Put aside all Adamic stories of creation
Forget about the *forbidden fruit* and the serpent
Face the reality
Who can deny to have come from a woman?
Isn't her body the gateway to life?
Who cares about this after seeing the light of day?
A few of course

How many of us do treasure such woman's importance
How many see her as an equal human
Is woman's future far more promising and certain?
How, if the so-called civilised world's never changed its vision
These are the issues we need to discuss and resolve
Doesn't the current view of a woman need deconstruction?
Doesn't it need decolonisation?
Let us face it as it truly is
A woman, like a man, is also human

A woman is not an object
Neither is she a property
That anybody can own
She needs to have her body as exclusively her own

59

She is not the property of the man
Be dad or husband
No community should own her
Doing so is belittling her
Stop objectification her
Respect her sanctity
Appreciate her sanguinity
Treasure her cordiality
Honour her sacrosanctity
Appreciate her equinity
What of her magnanimity?
Treat her just like any other
She is not that diffident
To the society she's like any other members
She is one of society manufacturers
This is a woman

Yes, I am talking about a woman
The one man likes to rule
Yes, it is the woman
A human
A wife
A daughter
A sister
A mother
Yes, a woman
Appreciate her input
Respect her humanity
Restore her dignity
Embark on parity
I see no dissimilarity

Between man and woman
Demonstrably, is this natural?
Nay
It is non-natural
What criminality

A woman is not a toy
Don't treat her like a yo-yo
For every bullyboy
Don't treat her like a batboy
Don't categorize her like a goy
Among the people of her own
She is not a property for anybody to own

Don't demonise her
Respect her
Treat her equally
Stop all infamy
By calling her a witch
Try to research the meaning of witch
Then compare it with the meaning of wizard
They are two different things
A witch is evil
A wizard is wonderful and smart
Why
Sexual discrimination
Gender formation

In some dogmas, women openly face discrimination
Even in the place of invocations
Women take back seats

Their faces are always concealed
Their voices are subdued
Their bodies are owned
Call this thingification if not objectification
In such brutal communities women are completely exploited
A man owns them like pitches
The man uses them like his fields
Despite its brutality this is called as culture
What sort of culture is this?
Do we need to preserve such a culture?

Despite such human degradation
We still talk about civilisation
To make matters even worse
We talk about equality
Which equality amidst sexual discrimination
What equality amidst sexual exploitation
Aren't female sold like produces
Isn't human traffic a booming business?
Where are women spared?
Is it in the West?
Nay, they too are exploited
Women are objectified
They are belittled though in a different way
Go watch their films
Aren't women depicted as flimsy?
Isn't their nudity exploited?
Doesn't the world fanatically love sex?
Who plays a great role between males and females?
Who supplies what and who gets what?

I know this can be misconstrued as libido to say
Yet, I know what to say
We may sometimes deny
We may curse and call it blasphemy
Whatever the names
This is what I see in the battle between sexes
This is what it is
Females are vexed
They are robbed
Robbed of their bodies
Robbed of their hearts
Simply because they are females
This is the only sin the created committed
Creating them females

This sin has been going on for a long stint
Yet, they call this modernity
Gender difference has become a reality
The tool by which males brutalise females
Some countries are now self-appointed double-faced
guardians of human rights
Which rights are these without gender parity?
How many female presidents do you know?
How many female monarchs do you know?
Their number is always slight
As the days go by it will plummet

As if it isn't enough, women are accompanied wherever they
go
They are monitored and told what to do
Regardless the fineness and finesse of what they do

Their credit goes to men
Who monitors the men?
Who spies on the lives of men?
Isn't this hypocrisy
Women are suspected of promiscuity
Do they do it alone really?
Women are deemed to be sexually weak
Again, is this accurate?
Ask yourselves who rushes when time comes
Between a woman and a man

Don't treat a woman like a coward
That needs your shield
Go to the borning room and see what she goes through
The time she bring the baby to the world
I am telling you she is tough enough
The pangs and tribulations she goes through
May sometimes speak volumes
I better emptyhandedly face ten lionesses
Than facing the pangs the expectant mother endures and
faces
How many do know this?

The woman is the source of our lives
This is what she is
This is what her permanent labour tells us
Yet, we don't appreciate this
No seed can geminate without facing death
The same way pregnant women face
It is a nine-month-between-death tryst
That perfects our lives

Is this a small feat?
Then why do we discriminate against women?
Why some cultures treat them like subhuman?
For how long will this go on?
It is time to do something about it
Let us do it right now wherever we are

Can flowers look down at leaves?
Which depends on another?
Without leaves a plant will starve
Without flowers the plant won't be pollinated
They all have functions to achieve
They need each other
None is better than another
Like tree's organs, humans depend on each other

Whether you are mighty or petty
You were all conceived by a woman
Wasn't Jesus conceived by a woman?
We are told Mary was this woman
Is she glorified on the tabernacle?
No, she gets a second mention
Why?
Simply because she is woman
You wonder the logic behind such discrimination
Judas Iscariot the traitor still enjoy a mention
Lucifer too is a more a celebrity than Mary
Why?
Because Mary is a woman

The clerk needs a sweeper

Without him or her
Streets will become a bomb
To diseases the residents will succumb
Even the doctor needs the sick persons
Will there be doctors without sick persons?
Will there be police without criminals?

Weren't apostles and prophets delivered by women?
Ironically, despite their important roles
Women have never given their deservedly prominence!
All prophets are men
Prophetesses are not heard of
Even where they existed
Their messages are not imparted
From them many are kept off

Who honours their sleepless nights for nine months?
Don't we take their labour for granted?
Aren't women unsung heroines
Add more sleepless of night breastfeeding
Add the pangs of nursing
Unsettled nights of wake-ups
Remember the dizziness they endure for months
Why don't we give them hands up?
Who pays all such chores they perform

Ants are small creatures
Remarkably, they are surrounded by wonders
Don't they magnificently erect anthills?
Aren't their houses air-conditioned without electricity
Despite such marvellous ability

They don't holler and claim a credit
They don't sing their mighty in science
Theirs has always been silence
They let our eyes see
They allow our brains to marvel and think
We need to take a stock
Of all things we take for granted

The stone is always deemed to be hard
Yet, water dissolves it
Though it take millions of years
At the end, the stone surrenders
It methodically wears out
Fire does boil water
To the point of evaporation
Interestingly, water easily douses fire
Which is stronger between the two?
Aren't they really equal?
The same applies to men and women
No one is better than another between the two

A hammer destroys the stone
Ironically, it comes from the same
They are all made from earth crust
Indeed, they are the creatures of dust
They are but soils though with different proportions
Their origin is the same
Though they carry different functions

If all men were women who would mould us

If all women were men what would have been the destiny of
men?
Don't we depend on each other like yin and yang?
Don't we complement each other?
Yes, we perfect each other
This is our nature
Equality is our nature
Though discrimination is becoming another culture

Teeth gnash food
Conversely, without taste buds no food can be eaten
Everything is indeed good
When all roles are appreciated
Some say fingers are not equal
They fail to underscore the roles they play
Fingers are equally on the stem
They all have important roles to play
Humans as well are equal
Even the roles they play are equally important
The high and mighty needs the *hoi polloi*
Without them there is no joy
In fact, the *hoi polloi* don't need the *hoity-toity*
The horse doesn't need the jockey
Such relationship lacks justice and equality

Do you think the high and mighty don't know their
dependence
They know everything per excellence
Thanks to their arrogance and ignorance
Yet, they still regard themselves as being matchless
They are ready to conceal everything

So that they can cling on fake mightiness

The bag does not need the money
Yet, the money needs the bag
The spoon doesn't need the mouth
For the mouth never fed the spoon
The spoon fills the mouth
While the mouth empties the spoon
Humans can't function like this
Spoons and mouths are things
We are human beings

Things do not to rebel
They don't even think
Should humans treat each other like things?
Doing so is heartlessness and folly
We need things surely
Hitherto, things don't need us
Humans need each other
To depend on each other
This is where the lesson of equality emanates and lies

How come the world fights for extinct animals
Hitherto, it keeps mum on gender abuses
How many years have we come from colonialism?
What have we done to bring gender egalitarianism?
As the so-called civilised world, aren't we still far from
realism?
How many females receive meagre salaries under
neoliberalism?
Some women are more educated than their counterpart men

Yet, their salaries are meagre simply because they are women
Many work diligently professionally and hard
Relentlessly, women have always worked for the world
In the farms
In the firms
Wherever they are, theirs is work
They work wholeheartedly for everybody
Ironically, they get no desirable reward
Why?
The reason is nothing but sexual discrimination
What is this if not utter foolishness?
Don't females need rights just like any humans?
Don't they have mouths to feed?
Don't they have tummy to fill?

Like any humans, women have feelings
So, too, they have valid needs
Sometimes, it become hard to understand
We discriminate against women based on their gender
Ironically, when it comes to sleeping
I see no exclusive women's beds
I see no distinct women's foods
When it comes to travelling
I see no women's exclusive roads
Isn't there any lesson in this?
Who looks at this like this?
The lesson is simple; sexual discrimination is a contradiction
It is the product of gullibility and exploitation

Sometimes back, women were not allowed to wear trousers
They fought and succeeded; and wore them

Is there anything that has practically changed?
All was the results of men's alarm
History is my witness
Women were prevented from working in offices
They fought and worked in offices
Is there anything males lost?
Nothing but their baseless fear at most

Gender is but socially constructed
Scientifically, it doesn't have any meaning
It also serves nothing
Except patriarchal hegemony

Women and men are carbon copies of each other
They need each other
They depend on each other
This is the rule of nature
Just imagine
Where would you be without this combination?
What would happen without this marvellous formulation?
When we talk about creation we mean this
It is behind human decision
Forever it will remain as it is
No doubt about it
This is the reality

Equally, humans yearn for some important things to them
One of them that causes nostalgia is home
Is there anybody who can define home?
Home means many things for many persons
Home is not the place one calls home

It is more than that
Home is those sounds, symbols and mystery that one knows
about a certain place
It is the place one arrived at and learned all things that person
knows
Those sounds
Those smells
The sounds of insects, trees, gorges, valleys and mountains
The rivers, lakes, deserts even ravines
They all make what we conceive as home
Everybody has a home be it developed or undeveloped
Everyone's home is unique and more valued than anything
one owns
You wonder why a person become nostalgic about the desert
He or she who was born in the desert
Nothing will outsmart the desert
For him or her, the desert is everything
He who was born in the forest,
Nothing will overvalue the forest
For him or her, the forest is everything
He/she who was born along the rivulet
Knows its beauties
The river is always bigger than a rivulet
But all have their beauties
In such an equation nothing is better or worse than another
They are all equal
They are home just like other things we tend to have and
treasure
Lemurs are unique to Madagascar just like Kangaroo are to
Australia

Song of my mother

This song is for my mother
Yes, it is for my comforter
The one who brought me here
The one who suffered for me
It is specially and exceptionally sung
It is sung for my mother
This is the song for my mother

I call upon you mother
Mother this is your song
It is the song of your son
It is the song of your daughter
It is the song of your offspring
Yes, the song
The song of your commemoration
The song of your commendation
Please listen to my sweet melody
I celebrate my realisation
Listen to my soliloquy

This song is for your mother
My mother
His mother
Her mother
Our mothers
All mothers of the world

There is no small mother

Neither is there a big mother
All mothers are mothers
Be they poor or wealthy
Be they sick or healthy
Be they educated or amateurish
All mothers are truly mothers

The song has no harmonica
It has no cymbals
It has no xylophone
It is the song of joy
The song has no cacophony
Yes, it is the song of appreciation
It is indeed the song of celebration
The song celebrates motherhood

Mom, I remember your exceptional love
True love
Unconditional love
You gave me what I have
Only God is the witness

You starved yourself for me
No way could you eat before I did
You fended for me
Even where you had nothing in hand
You kept fighting for me
To see me grow and become who I am

I remember your sufferings
Suffering from Hyperemesis Gravidarum

That morning sickness
Every pregnant woman suffers
You braved it mum
You deserve my praises

You taught me patience
Yes, patience is the mother of success
Nobody will ever succeed
If such a person lacks patience

The Song of my Father

Dad, like my mother, you have always been proud of me
You have offered your life for me
This has stuck with me
It is always intact in me
Thanks to your selfless and wisdom
Like your wife my mother
You equally stood by me
Let me sing you a song
The song of my honour
You know how tough it was to bring me up
Daddy, I will always give you thumbs up
Thanks for the heads-up
You always will be on the top on the slope
For the job well done
For the mission well accomplished
Thanks for what you did

Father, a disciplinarian *per se*
A man of no nonsense
Yours always is success
You wanted me to be successful
You wanted me to excel
In whatever I did
You wanted me to do it perfectly
Of all, you want me to excel

When you married my mother you didn't know me
You didn't even expect me

Nonetheless, you got me
You unassumingly and happily accepted me
Above all, you truly cared for me
You strongly fended for me
Thank you my hero, my daddy

I am yours by conviction but not by choice
Yet, I am yours not by force
You only chose one, my mom
Happily, with her you saw me through
You hanged tough
Even when it needed to do so through jabs
For me you could do
And you could do it without any ado
For, whatever that threatened me
You didn't jib
Defending me has always been your job

Aren't We Like Leaves?

All leaves are born vibrant
Again, their lives are but a stint
They blew in the wind like fans
To end up drying even if they live in fens

Aren't we like leaves?
When one is young looks down at elders
Slowly, it starts to sink in
That the way is the same by making
As one realises, it is dawn

Is there anybody that will live forever?
Aren't we like flowers?
Today, you are in your good shape
Tomorrow you are but an elderly

Every mother suffers twangs and pangs
When the baby arrives
The situation is the same in humans and animals
Yet, human laugh at animals!
Animals gape at humans
They wonder how crazy they are
They curse how selfish humans are
They kill each other
They hate each other
Animals don't know why
Humans too can't exactly tell why

Apart from being born, what happens when a person dies?
Humans may laugh at animals simply because they eat them
Should a lion laugh at a bunny?
Should the bunny laugh at the grasses?
When they die, aren't humans eaten by germs?
Isn't this a sign of equality of fate?
Only mother earth can laugh at us

Wisdom Towards Mother Earth

People love their jobs cars and castles
Then again
Who love a coffin?
Don't we spend tonnes of money on cars and castles?
Yet, when we die
The first thing to be thought about is nothing but a coffin
Wisdom has eluded many
Don't we pay many visits to churches, mosques and shops?
Who is the wise one that oft-visits the graveyard?
Aren't graveyards our permanent abode?
Who critically thinks about this?

We all came through the same way
Likewise, we will go the same way
For the trodden and the high and the mighty
We all will one day vanish and be taken away
Nothing will be left for and of us to cherish
Instead, others will cherish us
As they horribly wait for their turns
They will miss us
They will remember us
We will become history
Just like those who came before us
There will be nothing to blandish
There won't be any life to cherish
For, as we perish
We all will go to the no-go
This is our nature we who were born nude

Like fruits from the tree
Germs will mercilessly feed on us
Like flowers from the tree
The Sun will dry us
The crust will swallow us
We will be gone without any trace
Like flowers, we will fall
Like leaves, all of us will fall
Nobody will stand tall any more at all
When this very time knocks
Our beloved ones will yell
They will be gripped with pell-mell
With anguish, our beloved ones will yodel
Though, it will not change anything
Nothing will stop us from falling
Our beloved ones will wobble and yawl
Nothing will stop us from going
As come as go
This is the formula
Think about it

Being good to each other is all we need
Enthuse each other to do good things must be our creed
We need to shun individuality and greed
Our myopia will never do us good
We mortars are not of this world
Ours is no doubt a journey
The journey to the unknown
This journey does not need money
For one to reach the destination
We who were born nude

Do we know where water comes from?
Where do rivers go?
They go to the oceans
Where do oceans go?
Isn't life a sort of a merry-go-round?
Where is the true beginning of the world?
Where is its end?
Isn't the end the beginning and the beginning the end?
Sometimes, the end looks like the beginning
As well, the beginning looks like the end
However, there is the beginning and the end
Wherever we think we are improving
We end up finding
That we sadly are cascading
Aren't we destroying the world?
Aren't humans the great enemies of the world?
Isn't nuke science threatening the world?
Aren't we cascading in the name of advancing?
Who knows the end?
Who knows how it will look like?

We had no trace before we came
We will have a lot to leave when we leave
Yet, this is temporal
Time will erode everything
Nothing will be forever
However, we are books
Our lives are nothing but the chapters of the books
Those coming after us will read our books
The same we read the books of those before us
Our successors will analyse us

They will praise and condemn us
The same we did to those before us
How many will read our books
All depends on what we did right
A good legacy is a treasure
A bad legacy is loathsome

It saddens and shrinks my heart
Whenever I remember the end
It begs me to have guts and courage
Yet, fear always engulfs me
Trembling is me
As I explore the end
I swoop, seethe and lilt
Yet, it doesn't change anything
The end for everything is inexorable
For, the end is all about this book is about

Some books will never be read
They are as abhorrent as pukes
Their authors did not popularise them
Some will be read all over the world
Their authors were as popular as national anthems
Those will receive a mention
They will be read by millions
Our deeds are our books
The better the deeds
The more the readers
The worse the deeds
The less the readers
Who doesn't like his or her book to be read?

We need to create a good and an indelible mark wherever we
are
Our mission and work on earth must clearly show who we
are
Importantly, we must show that we care
Let our mission on earth be known everywhere
Yes, we need to care about every creature
The same those before us cared about us
They made the world what it is
Let our lives mean caring about others
This is why those who received us
Treated us
With the care we needed
Why can't we give back to those coming after us?

We need to get out of our cocoons
Let's work together for the coming generations
This is the only way we can appreciate our creation
We need to show that we were not an accident
Instead, we were a meaningful and success mission
In this light, there will be the fulfilment of our mission

To adequately thwart the dangers we face
We need to truly embark on climate justice
To do so, we need to act equally and decisively
We need to stand together globally
Forget about acting individually
We are facing the same danger equally
Stop thinking nationally
Instead, think internationally
Everything must be worked collectively

Our failures will be seen collectively
Our extinction will, as well, be experienced globally
The earth is one and one only
The modus to save it is also one only

Humans are now a big threat
Our actions are but numbing
Greed and myopia have taken control
Down in the abyss we always roll
With us on helms, the world faces a great peril
We are causing unbearable pangs
Everything has gone to dogs
We need to stand up for the future
Failure to which we are doomed

Aren't humans a threat to animals?
Aren't we a threat to ourselves?
Our knowledges about our dangers are miniscule
We are smaller than animals
When will we be able to see the looming peril?

We have made our lives needless difficult
By destroying the planet
Where will we go next?
Haven't our systems failed?
We need to understand and accept
There is no future without a healthy planet
We need to recalibrate our policies on environment
We need to stop our self-wiping out

Global warming has become a looming menace

Yet, we have ominously maintained our ignorance
We live in a state of denial
It is as if this isn't our sacrosanct business
The buck stops with us
And it is upon us
Everything is upon us
Therefore, it is our sole onus
To save our mother earth

Indeed, the future of this world is our serious business
For, nobody can plead any innocence
We all must be tasked for environmental delinquency
There is nothing more or less
Environmental culpability rests on human shoulders

Our resources are finite
They are quickly decreasing as we overconsume
As we pride that consumerism is development
There shall be no rebate
That we continue with our diabolic doom
Doomed is the entire humanity
What is left for and of us is to wise up
We need to strongly and unitedly stand up
Everybody must categorically say enow is enow
We must stop this self-inflicted blow

Out of selfishness
Out of our self-importance
There is a sure demise
Yes, the demise of humanity

Believe it or not
Out of our ignorance
Remember
Nobody will make it
Nobody will win this battle
Unless we all change our ways
Destruction is real
Everybody must heed this
The writings are on the wall for us
We who were born nude
Born nude as I have explored it
It is nothing but a reminder and symbol of our equality
Likewise, our humanity hangs on this fact
That we all were born nude
Nude we were born
Empty handed we came
Likewise, empty handed we will go
Without any fame we came
Likewise without it, we will go
Weak we arrived
We will leave
Whatever we made and treasured will be left behind
Our cars, dreams, houses and loved ones
All will be left behind
We will go to where we came from
Where we came from we will return
Born nude
Yes, born nude
Nude we were born